God's Goodness

GOD'S GOODNESS

Franklin Atkinson

BROADMAN PRESS
Nashville, Tennessee

4215-23
ISBN: 0-8054-1523-8

Dewey Decimal Classification: 231.8
Subject heading: GOD
Library of Congress Catalog Card Number: 80-66228

Printed in the United States of America

Dedicated to
My cherished companion Barbara
and our children
Ruth, Jean, and David
whose marvelous qualities
have made a delightful home
in which these studies have grown

Preface

These studies are intended for serious students of the sacred Scriptures. The ideal combination for presenting materials has been attempted: a popular style to permit continuous reading in order to understand most easily the discussion, plus the isolating of technical data in footnote form to give supportive evidence easily in view. This collection of technical and reference information is designed to assist those who might not have easy access to it, but who could personally enjoy and profitably use it.

These materials should stimulate personal devotion with both delight and benefit. In addition, they may be used for studies in regular church services (sermons, devotions), for certain interest groups; for retreats for adults, youth, and pastors, and possibly for other specifically interested audiences.

Acknowledgments

Grateful acknowledgment for permission to quote material from other publications is extended to the following: *The Saturday Evening Post Company* for excerpts from "The New Fears of J. Paul Getty" by Joy Billington; Baker Book House for material from *The Acts of the Apostles* (1979 paperback edition) by Richard B. Rackham; Word Music, Inc., Winona Lake, Indiana, for the African Folk Song, "God Is So Good," used by permission.

Scripture quotations marked ASV are from the American Standard Version of the Bible.

Contents

1   *God Is Good—Always!* 11
2   *God Is Good—Really* 21
3   *Disputed by Satan* 29
4   *Contradicted by Sin* 35
5   *Radiated in Redemptive Hope* 45
6   *Demonstrated by Persistent Love* 51
7   *Foundation of His Goodness: The Divine Names* 71
8   *Revealed by the Personal Name* 79
9   *Shown by the Unique Personal Presence* 89
10 *Disclosed by Descriptive Titles* 101

   Notes 115

1
God Is Good—Always!

Genesis 1

Floundering in confusion, a hurting humanity searches vigorously for a hope. Haunted and hungering hearts stumble in perplexity in the recognition of the extensive truth-scandals of sex and other dishonesty among prominent leaders of our nation. Heralds of "Roads to Recovery" are numerous.

Yet our people need to know that a person's evaluation of his god (God) will determine his character and conduct. That is why the basic reality of the one true God deserves notice throughout society.

The fascinating factual history of the rose named "Peace" exhibits the insatiable craving of the whole twentieth century. A breeding program was begun in 1935 with the purpose of creating a hardy, copper-colored rose with robust and decorative foliage. Originating in France, budwood was sent to Germany and Italy in 1939, the year that World War II began. The experimental product, still unnamed, was smuggled to the United States later that year, arriving on the very day (or the day after) Germany threatened to sink any United States ship that entered the war zone. The horticultural authorities named this outstanding rose "Peace" to express the world's greatest desire. Amazingly, the historical progress of this rose matched the march of the world toward that supreme goal—peace. The Pasadena Rose Show, with the date chosen in advance, was selected as the place to proclaim officially the name of the rose. That date turned out to be the day that Berlin fell.

It is interesting to note, too, that when the United Nations Conference met in San Francisco in 1945, intent on finding a means for maintaining peace in the world, the American Rose Society voted to let "Peace" make its first public appearance there. The date was decided. Roses needed to be produced, of course, to the right stage of blooming, and they had to be transported and distributed to the Conference delegates on the precise date. All went as planned. Each United Nations delegate discovered in his hotel room a "Peace" rose. That date was VE Day!

Even more excitement is entwined with the unusual history of this rose. Dates for announcing the All-America winners are set months in advance so that the declaration can be made simultaneously around the world. In the year 1945, "Peace" was the only rose which won the honor; and the report resounded around the world on what became VJ Day. Also, on a predetermined date, the American Rose Society presented its gold medal to "Peace." And, appropriately enough, that was the date the treaty was signed with Japan!

This clamoring for peace calls for the realization that God is always good, a basic, significant concept that will delightfully determine one's whole philosophy of life. But mankind possesses a subconscious suspicion against God. Perhaps he is *not* totally good and wanting good for us. This destructive element is seen in our frantic efforts to explain tragedy as "God's will," or our serving unhappily in a situation, even with fears and regret, but dutifully as "the will of the Lord." If one would express honestly his thoughts about certain circumstances, he would admit, "It hurts. I don't like it. I'd change it if I could. But I must submit to the will of God, dreadfully." And some determine whether or not they are following the

Master's will by the degree of "dedicated misery." However, the same consecrated surrender can be made in sweet confidence that his will is intended for good to us or to others through us. "Come over and help us" from Macedonia seemed questionable to Paul while in torture and pain; yet it was sweet realization that God's good was within his knowledge to perform.[1]

Individuals need to punch a correction for their computer-like subconsciousness to print: "God is good—always!" Genesis 1—2 reveals this truth which is so succinctly stated in 1 John 4:8: "God is love." That is his very nature, not a remembrance to be polite in actions when with others.

With tremendous skill the literary artist indicated that everything God both created and developed was good. One such indication is the designed purpose of fulfillment for every object that he created. When this is understood, it will breathe renewed vitality to many of God's own today. But too few have opportunity to see this magnificent purpose of the Almighty.

Purposeful provisions for personal growth to fulfillment has always been the very nature of God's creative activity. Such is a major hunger of sincere saints. This achievement is obviously a paramount need for contemporary Christianity.

It is emphasized in New Testament compulsion.[2] But it has remained hidden to so many as the normal purpose of God expressed meticulously and wonderfully in the Genesis creation account.

This marvelous purpose of God can be detected by careful concentration on Genesis 2:3. A deliberate distinction is made between the terms "create" and "made."[3] The Hebrew text heightens the expectation by having a construction of purpose, literally rendered, "which he had created *for making*."[4] The stimulating testimony of God's creative activity emphasizes the purpose of definite development to fulfillment—even our spiritual life, "the image of God!" God is so good to endow his purposes for our achievement.

God's efforts for mankind's spiritual progress is the subject of the Bible. Genesis 1—2 skillfully introduces it with precise grammar. Yet the careful student will discover delightfully in his English translations this glorious truth so often unobserved. If one will mark the exact listing of "create," he will note a sparing usage. Actually, only three distinct "creative" acts are recorded in Genesis 1.

Each involves what only God can create, and he creates each without use of anything existing at the time. Excitement thrills the believer when he sees for himself that the Bible lists "creation" only to be (1) the material world substance (Gen. 1:1); (2) the animal "soul" or "living principle" (Gen. 1:21); and (3) the "image of God" in man and woman (Gen. 1:26-27).

Then, with delicate deliberateness the writer proceeds to show that the Almighty, in loving purpose, directed the orderly growth of every "created-from-nothing" item by using forces and materials that had been brought into existence.[5] This matchless attention by the immanent God to every element of his "creation" assures us of such interest and effort for growth of our spiritual lives, the created "image of God."[6]

That he attempts to shape us by use of existing forces, factors, and circumstances enhances the assurances of Romans 8:28. The subject of that marvelous verse is technically the indefinite, impersonal "all things" used with the verb of action, "works."[7] Moreover, the confidence of his continuing the developing of us is declared: "He who began a good work in you will perfect it until the day of Jesus Christ" (Phil. 1:6, ASV). This has always been his practice from Genesis onward.

The goodness of God in the creation account is repeatedly stated: "And it was good" or "God saw that it was good." To many readers the statements are so repetitious as to border on monotony; however, such emphasis delights the devoted person who appropriates God's similar interest and efforts in him.

The one situation that God declared "not good," he proceeded to provide (Gen. 2:18), and the greatness of God's achievement to help man is realized by several truths. For example, the description for woman is more significant than a usual translation of "help-meet" or " helper." The writer described her as "a help corresponding to him."[8] This recognizes a being far superior to mere femaleness. She was of much greater worth than being merely a sex-partner. She was to be of the same exalted character and spiritual capacities as the man. The personality factors, indicating distinct difference from animals, are indicated in the change of terms used from *adam* for "man" to *ish*.[9]

This goodness of God to provide equal partners magnifies man's happiness. When joy comes, delight is doubled. When a burden arrives, it is divided and becomes only half as heavy. So, the dramatic description of an ideal marital relationship is often stated as follows: the Almighty did not take woman from man's foot, indicating that he could degrade or mistreat her. However, neither did he take her from man's head, permitting her to dominate him. The wise Creator correctly removed a rib from man's side to make his partner, his companion: from his side that they could support each other, from beneath his arm to be protected and provided for by him, and from near his heart to be loved by him.

Insights into the early activities of God compound the evidence of his goodness. Even his commands were and are for human good. The positive command to till the ground was beneficial. The Lord's prohibition was prompted by the goodness of God to protect man and so declared "lest ye die."

God's goodness continued to be exposed as he provided mankind with the capacity for choice in moral and spiritual matters (Gen. 2:9). Adam and Eve understood the privileges and options (Gen. 3:2-3). They enjoyed the satisfaction of successful spiritual growth in relation to choices and deliberate exercise of personal control: will. These methods for developing character and strong moral fibers are with us also as expressions of our Master's goodness to permit our development.

In addition, God's magnificent goodness was exhibited in the divine-human communion encounters. Spiritual stimulation, personal guidance, perceptive insights, and detection of divine wisdom all enhanced the luxury of living with a good God. Such opportunities enjoyed by Adam and Eve are with us—they came during the course of living, working, deciding in a material world. A major victory for us can be in reconstructing our evaluations to realize that God is good—always! The song declares:

> God is so good,
> God is so good,
> God is so good,
> He's so good to me.

AFRICAN FOLK SONG

2
God Is Good—Really

Genesis 2—3

Would you be surprised if you peeked into your subsconscious being and discovered a hesitant suspicion of God? Do you construct life with a confidence that he is really good? Some individuals reserve complete surrender from him, wondering what he might require them to do, or where he might send them to serve if they did not protect themselves.

Our tendency toward negativism opens avenues for destructive suggestions against God. Decisions are often made on assumptions. For example, on October 20, 1966, the police of New Orleans, Louisiana, searched an hour and a half in the 17th Street Canal for a "drowning victim." An off-duty policeman and another motorist reported they saw a man jump from the Interstate bridge about 7:00 AM. The "victim" was found at his office at work. But, truthfully, he did jump from the bridge, as he did each morning, to a ledge about four feet away. He walked across a huge pipe to catch the city bus directly across the way; it saved him a long walk, or drive, via city streets. Circumstantial appearances can be wrong so often.

Bewildered individuals reflect with serious alarm as to how or why they yielded to Satan's intrigue. This appeal of suspicion against God's basic goodness is a primary tactic of Satan. Being informed and alert to it is a vital defense.

Contrast the lovely garden atmosphere with the turbid turmoil in the soul of the guilty pair of Genesis 3. The blazing beams of sun had receded in late afternoon, leaving only the golden splendor of rays shooting into the western sky. The gentle breezes kept kissing God's creation with tender, cooling touches. Conditions invited repose, relaxation, and the customary divine-human communion. But, in the innermost reality of the cringing couple burst the blistering blaze of guilt, scorching its way into the sensitive souls of Adam and his bride. Calm communion had been traded for frenzied fright that stabbed into their distraught minds. Fractured fellowship had tightened the tension by winding man's emotional constitution into unusual discord.

Probably the pair wondered, *How could it possibly be?* The answer begins with a question mark. The serpent's wording of 3:1 denotes something surprising or unexpected, that is to say, "Has God *really* said...?"[1] The force of the question was far from an honest inquiry for information. Designed to instill some element of doubt, it planted that negative seed of suspicion: "Did God really say exactly that?" "Did God really intend such restriction?" "Could you have misunderstood what God really wanted?" Divine goodness was the target of the sinister insinuation.

The serpent had entered with the contagious suspicion of negative reflection against divine goodness. Then the crafty being continued to lead the progression of doubt. Additional fuel to propel the now interested one's thoughts of mystery detection was injected in Satan's following assurance. Implication of divine selfishness or jealousy as the reason for a lying threat about death directed her shaken confidence from the Creator to the critic.

The process continues to succeed with citizens of our society. Rational, reasonable solutions cannot always be given to objections against divine instructions about character building or problems of consistency. But strength is available in the conviction that God is good—really!

Divine goodness expressed itself in efforts to lift the fallen victims. God's question ("Where are you?") was not for his information. But to receive the tendered reclamation, the fright-filled couple must realize where they were spiritually. Goodness sought them.

Capture the trauma by reconstructing the next presentation of divine goodness (3:14-19). The paramount thrust was the first note of redemptive hope, often called the *Protevangelium*. The announcement of divine determination to intervene on behalf of his people was directed to the serpent, but it was spoken in the audience of the couple. Such thoughtfulness of God!

The background was their terrifying touch of temptation. They were engulfed in suffocation of sin. Enclosed with dark, drab drapes of despair, they floundered for release. There they stood—wrapped in the gray, ghostly garments of guilt. They had been captured by counterfeit fame. Surely, each shivered in the cold, clammy climate of conscience. She had been snared by the snake. The fear-filled friends in frustration must stand with bare nakedness of soul, no adequate excuse.

The immediate foreground was man's just, deserving prospect of punishment. The future proposed a bleak, barren desert of the spiritual life. Separation from their Creator-Companion intensified the loneliness of lostness. The blissful garden had been exchanged for the blight of thorns and thistles. Communion had been relegated to the place of insignificance with respect to God's words of wisdom and guidance. The pair remained in the arena of experience, clutching the shattered promises of Satan.

Impending judgment appeared in man's crystal ball of expectation. The swinging sword symbolized suicide. The "electric chair" of justice waited to welcome the cringing couple. *Then* the goodness of God brought the bright, brilliant beams of redemption. Satan was pronounced judged, and his defeat was predicted. God still loved the sinners and would enter the warfare, assuring them victory. Suspicion must melt before assurance. God is good—really!

It will be surprising to some because they have not noticed it; it may seem strange to others because it is judicial; but it is stimulating to others because it, too, discloses God's goodness. The expulsion from the Garden, with the entrance protected by the flaming sword, was exceedingly merciful. The marvelous truth is difficult to see because the peculiar, grammatical construction is scarcely used in English. Most readers pass over it (Gen. 3:22). The sentence is simply chopped off, an incomplete expression. The thought was contemplated, the condition raised; then the possible result was suppressed, abandoned. Apparently, it was too terrible to consider seriously. And, intelligent use of privation proclaims his goodness.[2]

Several factors were involved. Humankind's redemption, with its several constituents, basically was at stake. To have to live forever in the horrible haunts of guilt, fear, and broken communion, realized in the first flush of the sinful entanglement, would have been torment indeed. But to sense the necessity of forgiveness and reclamation, man must experience the reality of his wrong. Expulsion made a dramatic impact. Thus, twentieth-century man also will not repent until he sees his need because of his separation from God. Disturbing conviction is God's love in action.

Moreover, that God maintained authority of the tree of life, man's redemption, shows his goodness. If mankind had "manipulated" God, or wrested from his control access to the Garden, unlimited chaos would have surely engulfed the

world if dominated by man's desires. The Genesis
account so wisely depicts this story as introductory to Cain's sinful self and his ancestors and to
the urgent realization of man's need " to call upon
the name of Jehovah" (4:26, ASV).

3
Disputed by Satan

Genesis 3

After capturing our attention by an emphatic positioning of words, the inspired writer dramatically introduced the tempter, Satan. Normal Hebrew order is to emphasize the action by placing the verb first in the sentence. Here, however, "the serpent" is located first in the sentence. Obviously, he is a major character in this drama.

A significant interpretative decision is necessary concerning "the serpent." The writer of Genesis did not give it (him) a name or a title. To let the passage speak for itself, we must not assume that here we have "Satan" or the devil. "Serpent" is the only description the author employed. Four evidences related to that being indicate that someone greater than a snake is involved here. First, it (he) possessed unusual superior knowledge about the following data:

God's instruction to Adam and Eve, the result of sin in opening their eyes in experience, and the psychology of enticement. Second, his power of human speech (or intellectual communication) proposes something beyond an ordinary snake. Third, the elements of personality become evident: mental reasoning ability and volitional choice ("because thou hast done this," v. 14). Fourth, the enmity declared by the Almighty is used of "person" enemies throughout the Old Testament. The Hebrew word is regularly used of people, not of animals which were nonresponsible morally. Moreover, this personal warfare was to continue between the seed of woman, which would be persons, and the seed of the serpent, which must define beings as other than natural snakes.

This forceful introduction of this exceedingly clever personality catches our attention for our personal alertness. Athletic teams regularly scout opponents in order to effect a good defense. The apostle Paul enjoined us to follow his practice when he wrote as follows: "lest Satan should get an advantage of us: for we are not ignorant of his devices" (2 Cor. 2:11). Thus, to alert, to warn, and to convince ourselves of his destructive intentions will benefit us immensely. This recorded experience provides us illumination of his destructive devices and degraded character.

But many people fail to sense the seriousness of
Satan. A comedian regularly could get laughs
with his claim, "The devil made me do it." The
newspapers reported that a couple in California
asked the blessings of Satan upon their wedding
in a "Satanist church." A court in Finland had to
decide what to do with a will which stated that a
man's farm was to be deeded to the devil. Com-
temporary fascination with Satan worship,
demons, and spirits depict the general populace's
lack of understanding of the power of the
seriousness needed in regard to this group. The
headline, "Pope Voices Concern Over Satanist
Cults," appeared in newspapers all over the
world. The Pope was quoted as saying: "We all
are under an obscure domination . . . . It is by
Satan, the prince of this world, the No. 1 enemy."

I. Satan Attacked the Goodness by Deception

The introductory statement specifically
declared that this serpent was "subtle." The
Hebrew word means "skillful, wise, alert, clever,
and such mental excellence." This fact explains
his extraordinary ability to entice and to convince. By three discernible approaches Satan
tricked Eve. First, he presented himself unfairly

as a friendly, helpful advisor. But he cleverly stimulated her suspicion of the goodness of God's word by inquiring: "Did God *really* say...?" He could also be shaking her self-confidence in her understanding of God's instructions. He was mean and cruel to undermine the truth of good instructions intended to protect mankind from death. He was bad to take advantage of Eve's inexperience with such a sinister being. Later evaluation of this crafty creature would describe him and his followers as false and deceitful: "For Satan himself is transformed into an angel of light" (2 Cor. 11:13-14), when in reality he is an agent of darkness.

A second attack was Satan's implication that God was selfish and unreasonable (v. 5). He led Eve to believe that God could not share his exalted position with the couple who would become comparably elevated if they proceeded to disobey God.

Then third, with an authoritative assurance, Satan guaranteed Eve that they would not certainly die. His cruel meanness was exhibited by his deliberate lie. Jesus would later explicitly explain the devil as follows: "He . . . abode not in the truth, because there is no truth in him. When he speaketh a lie, he speaketh of his own; for he is a liar, and the father of it" (John 8:44).

II. Satan Attacked the Goodness by Destruction

Satan is destructive by nature. He enjoys it; he likes to see people hurt. The way of degradation and the destroying of ideals, character, and souls is natural with him. Jesus declared quite forcefully: "He was a murderer from the beginning" (John 8:44). Our people need to realize that we cannot expect any permanent good to come from Satan. Nothing of benefit to us can ever be produced by cooperation or compromise with him.

Satan's nature of cruelty and destructiveness is revealed by the descriptive word *subtle*. Although the Hebrew word does mean wise, clever, intelligent, and alert, it also has another possible meaning. It was used also of cruelty in torture which would result in slow death. The Arabic cognate was used to describe the tearing of flesh from the bones, the stripping of leaves from trees, and the removing of bark from trees that they slowly, but surely, die. Hence, Satan is bad by nature; he is a natural destroyer. Consequently, man, by himself, can never win in dealings with the devil.

4
Contradicted by Sin

Genesis 3

"Where to Sin in San Francisco" was the title of a booklet in a hotel lobby. One shudders at the possibly unlimited enticements of wrong until he examines the contents of the booklet. Then he responds with fright that sin is considered so trifling, for the booklet is only a guide to more famous restaurants and theaters of the city. We even joke about sin! People discuss "little" sins and "big" sins; they estimate one action's degree of wrong in order to justify the indulgence of another.

Glances at news reports by popular magazines of surveys and evaluations easily convince one of a commonly accepted sin-saturated society. So our examination of the entrance of sin into our world should be highly instructive. It should be of great significance because every avoided element of sin should be an asset in one's character.

I. DEFINITION

Disobedience of God is the plain, basic, and real definition of sin. The source is the heart (choice-making device) of mankind. But the encounter with Satan by Eve can help us detect similar steps which lead to that decisive, deliberate decision.

Satan's first attack was a slanted question to instill *doubt.* Perhaps Eve interpreted it to be an honest inquiry since she had never met such a lying creature. The use of the Hebrew word *pen* indicates an insinuation with a deprecatory force if spoken with alarm or suspicion. The goal of Satan would certainly verify such vocalization. Inherent in the question could have been hints of insinuations such as, "Did God *really* say . . . ?" or "Did God dare to mean . . . ?" or "Did God say truly or did you misunderstand?" Doubt of God's good intentions for them was basic in the approach. Satan implied that God was unduly restricting them because of some bad motive in God: perhaps he was selfish in refusing to share honors or equality with mankind, or perhaps God was a domineering tyrant who was fearful of losing control over these subjects if their eyes were truly opened by the revolt experience.

The fertile seeds of suspicion were nurtured by

the concentration on the negative, the prohibition. Eve admitted that God had provided fruit of
other trees of the Garden. But, likewise, we
habitually reduce notice of our blessings and
multiply the size of our restrictions, disappoint-
ments, and mistreatments.

Doubling the degree of doubt, Satan cleverly
declared assurance that Eve was evaluating correctly. He guaranteed that "You will not surely
die." She enjoyed being "sold" or convinced that
she had made the intelligent decision. Correspondingly, we react similarly. So, Satan bravely
attacked the motive of God, even his goodness (v.
5). He proposed that God restrained them because
of selfish pride which refused to share prestige.
Satan indicated that when Eve became liberated
by the disobedience, she would be better, she
would know more, and she really would be more
like God—probably in knowledge and authority.

Doubt instilled by Satan, then as well as now,
found its strength in half-truths. Eve did not die
physically in that twenty-four-hour day. And, her
eyes were opened (to the experience of sin) as God
admitted (v. 22). Such partially good elements
often do confuse our evaluations. Because these
good-bad distinctions are difficult to determine in
many situations, we must have God's illumina-

tion and evaluation. But see the age-old deceptive presentations by the liquor industry. They claim that law can't keep everyone from drinking anyway. So they propose that it be easily accessible to all. Then they suggest that better health conditions to the drinker would be obtained if liquor were made in the inspected, hygienic processes rather than makeshift home hideaways. Also, they figure that the liquor industry can produce tax revenue for education of the young and welfare for the aged. And it does pay taxes; the reports merely fail to indicate the additional, excessive costs to society beyond the industry's tax payments.

Another example of the popularity of half-truth approaches to entice people is the prostitution proposal of 1976 in Nevada. The supportive arguments match those employed by the liquor industry. First, prostitution can't be stopped. Some people are going to indulge. Second, legalization would provide better health conditions and stop the spread of venereal disease. Third, we all might as well earn tax funds from the registered business. Fourth, legalization won't affect the nonusers, so they should not deprive users of their privileges. One extremely liberal congregation in Texas proposed that the state legislature should legalize and control prostitution "which would make exploitation of the profession by criminal elements impossible."

Doubts build in the minds of some good citizens from such half-truths. The entrance of suspicion about God's goodness and wisdom is potentially devastating.

A second significant step leading to the real stroke of disobedience is *desire*. The reasonableness of the logic in the half-truth approach granted Eve permission to continue considering the possibility of partaking. God's good provision had been abundantly sufficient. But man wanted more.

Eve discovered that the forbidden did have three appeals which are sometimes good, and, therefore, justifiable (v. 6). The universal and timeless aspects of these approaches to Eve are evident in that Satan used those same three in the recorded temptations of Jesus and will use them against us according to 1 John 2:15-16. That fruit "was good for food" (ASV). Our bodies are made to live by food. Jesus fed the people food miraculously. "So," she possibly concluded, "it must be all right—just forbidden."

But the lesson our citizens need to learn is that sometimes sin is using good things wrongly.

Although Jesus fed the hungry and taught his disciples to refrain from worrying about food, he rejected Satan's temptation to make bread for himself from stones (Matt. 4:4). Also, the "lust of the flesh" is a primary source for temptation in a materialistic world (1 John 2:16). Likewise, the natural desires and drives of our bodies remain good only when directed by divine guidelines. Sexuality is an example in our day.

A second item which prompted a continuation of Eve's leaning toward the acceptance of the forbidden was that "it was a delight to the eyes" (ASV). The thrill of beauty through the sense of sight is terrific. "So," Eve possibly reasoned, "what could be wrong with it?"

The expression "pleasant to the eyes" can describe her emotional thrill. This experience could be either wholesome or degrading for anyone. Emotions hold friendships, homes, and loyalties together. On the other hand, excitement in vulgarity can be a genuine emotional response through sense perception. So, a second mention of "worldliness" is stated in 1 John 2:16 as "the lust of the eyes" (ASV). Practical expressions of the emotional involvement in destructive influence by this medium are lewdness of literature, movies, television, kinds of clothing, and language. Magazines which display naked bodies are in great demand. An individual can gain an emotional thrill by the provocation of his imagination by pictures or literary descriptions.

Jesus confronted the "pleasant-to-the eyes" enticement from Satan as recorded in Matthew 4:6. Spectacular acclaim with its inherent emotional delight was suggested if Jesus would plunge from the Temple steeple and be rescued in flight by angels. Of course, the Master detected the trap and rejected it.

The third half-truth element employed to heighten Eve's desire was that the fruit would make one wise. The Hebrew word *sakal* means "to be prudent, understanding, skillful" and also "to prosper or to have success." The ambition to succeed often propels one beyond the mere mental achievements of "being wise." Thus the larger concept was probably included in Eve's estimations.

Obviously, the drive to succeed can be good and wholesome. Scriptures indicate divine approval for work and thrift. But the deceptive half-truth lures many people into a dungeon of sinful cravings to prosper, regardless of the guidance of God, moral character, or inevitable results. Satan tried it on Jesus: instant success of world ownership (Matt. 4:10). Jesus conquered the appeal by substituting the wise involvement in worship and service of the Lord.

Likewise, John wrote that "the pride of life" is a normal allurement into worldliness away from God (1 John 2:16). Such desire easily leads to deliberate disobedience, especially when it has emerged from suspicions and doubt of God's absolute goodness.

The real, decisive definition of sin is *disobedience,* which is a form of rebellion. This fatal step was taken by Eve as stated in Genesis 3:6. It involves an evaluation of God. The deep disposition of an individual to live contrary to God's will as expressed by God's statements is what sin actually is. Sin is an attitude of evaluation. It is a response of the intellect as evidenced by the possession of knowledge about God's will (vv. 2-3). The reaction of personal choice to disobey God is deliberate, though perhaps not violent.

The responsibility of guilt is therefore absolutely individual. Each one, Adam and Eve, was designated as a participant by the writer as he stated that Eve ate and that Adam also ate. Indicating that the punishment was based on a personal choice, God said, "Because thou hast hearkened . . . and hast eaten" v. 17). Mankind attempts to shift responsibility to someone else, but God retains responsibility upon each individual.

The terrifying consequences include divine punishment such as that expressed in Genesis 3:14-19. Yet, inescapably, some effects of sin are internal; they include the horrors of guilt (v. 8) and fear (v. 10). The evident separation from communion with God is also an immediate and definite result of disobedience. Thus, man's defection from alliance with God in his goodness is certainly to man's detriment. However, God's goodness is sustaining and enriching.

5
Radiated in Redemptive Hope

Genesis 3

Sin! Guilt! Fright! Who cared? He whom they feared! Our world, like Adam and Eve, finds it surprising that the holy God who extremely hates sin loves the sinner limitlessly. He presented to the undeserving couple their first ray of redemptive hope.

The extremity of his goodness can be recognized if the reader will reconstruct the scene by vivid imagination. The stark disobedience of man must be comprehended in order to realize the greatness of the character of God.

Observe the background of this proclamation of love—man's deliberate experience in sin. Confusion captured the reasoning abilities of Adam and Eve because their disobedience did not produce the success that Satan had assured. Tension twisted their emotional constitution because their happiness had turned into horror. Their independence had become slavery, and their dreams had regressed into nightmares. Life changed to death; despair conquered their expectations. Perplexity dominated their volitional faculties. Their convincing confidant had trapped them. He also had apparently deserted them. The lights of their souls had been extinguished. The stunning consequences of morbid fear and unexplainable guilt gripped every facet of their being. The dark, dismal drapes of despair enclosed them.

The foreground of the proclamation was correspondingly void of hope. Their future beckoned them to enter the era of loneliness, a separation from that wonderful companion who visited them in the cool of the day. They might be furiously active and be encircled by scores of people, but they would be secretly and desperately lonely. They even had traded the blissful garden for barrenness with thorns and thistles.

The immediate prospects displayed the certain punishment of the flaming sword at the gate of the Garden. That swinging sword signified suicide. Their crystal-ball prediction could only offer impending judgment. What an achievement for the intelligent, self-sufficient pair!

Who cared? Their merciful God revealed his character when all other hope had vanished. Ever so timely was his goodness exhibited. In *their* presence he dealt with Satan just when they needed it most. This was refreshing and encouraging. God was dependable in ability and desire to conquer their foe.

A purposeful plan is evident in this early promise of redemption, often called protevangelium. The disclosure that the serpent was indeed a person was made by God's placing volitional responsibility on him. "Because you have done this" is an emphatically placed clause describing the justice deserved by Satan. This justice includes both a curse and a prophecy. The "lowdownness" and crookedness stated in the curse would apply to the person of Satan as well as to the embodiment of the serpent. Actually, since a difficulty is obvious in the punishment of the snake family inasmuch as they were involuntarily used by Satan, we would see the primary emphasis of the curse to be on the degradation of Satan, the person of choice. Therefore, our confidence in the Almighty can be confirmed because he maintains authority over our chief enemy. Doubtless, that realization stimulated hope in Adam and Eve.

The love-expressing God proceeded to describe his plan with the declaration of continued conflict. The term "enmity" tells of warfare between persons. The fact that the confrontation could exist through the ages reflects another stimulus of encouragement to mankind; Satan cannot conquer us completely. The personal instigation by the Almighty of such conflict reveals his participation with us. For he said, "I will put enmity . . ." (v. 15). To designate the woman as humanity's specific representative would restore her sense of worth and acceptance since she had been the leader into rebellion.

In addition, persistent progress is expected. The character of God provides dependable endurance to success. So ultimate victory is declared. The pronouns "he" and "you" are placed emphatically in the Hebrew text. The antecedent of "he" would be the seed of woman since God was speaking directly to Satan, the pronoun "you." Satan will inflict pain and damage as referred to by an attack on man's heel. But such injury need not be fatal. On the other hand, the blow to Satan's head would be a crushing defeat—death.

Inasmuch as no element of humanity can conquer Satan, this prediction inherently implies "the Son of Man" to be the Victor. Historical references contain notices of those confrontations between Satan and Jesus. The multiplied tempta-

tions, the devilish attempts on Jesus' life to prevent the cross experience, and the compounded
discouragements near the end of his ministry
disclose the fierce struggles of the two com-
batants. The victory of Jesus' death-resurrection
experience sealed Satan's doom. He has been
judged; he awaits the final sentence.

Oh, how God loves these sinners! He exposed
this first promise of redemptive hope when life for
Adam and Eve was extremely empty. He has continued to express his goodness to mankind to us
of the present. He eagerly desires our favorable
response to accept his forgiveness and his
presence.

6
Demonstrated by Persistent Love

Genesis 4

"Oxford Scholar Dies on Bowery Skid Row," declared the headline of the two-column newspaper report. "Professor," age 62, the Bowery's "most illustrious citizen," was dead. The proud professor was an authority on English romantic poetry. He had earned his Ph.D. from Oxford University and had been earning a splendid salary teaching in a college in New York. But he had been fired from his teaching position because of his romantic escapades involving students and faculty wives. He landed on the Bowery in a district known as "One Mile of Hell." The news account reported that "an assortment of shabbily clothed panhandlers and winos gathered at Mike's Bar . . . toasting a departed comrade."

When anyone sees such tragedy strike a relative, friend, or merely a stranger, he discovers that two questions crash into his mind: (1) What causes a person to do such a thing? and (2) Who did anything to prevent it? The detailed account of Cain's experience vividly describes the route to a ruined life. Obviously the purpose for preserving the story was more than to account for the first child. The Bible does not continue a discussion of his descendants; so, apparently, its inclusion in sacred records is to demonstrate some aspect of the character of Jehovah and the response of mankind to him (Gen. 4:26).

A careful reading of this report will reveal the persistent, pursuing love of God seeking to reach the rebellious sinner by several different approaches. Lessons to be learned from Cain's sad destruction indicate that there is a progression related to sin: (1) deeper and deeper entanglement, (2) a hardening of responsiveness, and (3) a degrading direction toward destruction. Items within the text itself will expose answers to the two initial questions from Cain's experience. Although the biblical record shows the interrelation of Cain's continual journey in sin with Jehovah's persistent pursuit of love, this exposition will separate them for clarity in answering those two disturbing questions stated above.

The very first factor that started his tragic episode was that of omitting God from his life.

This report consistently used the personal name "Jehovah" to report divine dealings with Cain. The basic heart response to Jehovah is intimated in Genesis 4:3. The Hebrew preposition, **min**, expresses separation or partitive actions, "from, out of." Cain merely took "some" from his produce, not mindful of quality or amount as would befit an expression of adoration in worship. *Just anything*, he thought, *would get the offering task completed.* The act was nothing more than a superstitious bribe, as happens in every era; and it revealed a condition of his spiritual life, his religious neglect.

The deeper-than-surface reverence is exposed by Abel's meticulous selection of the best, first, and fattest, as a heart expression of devotion. Later evaluation verifies the early diagnosis that absence of faith was Cain's problem (Heb. 11:4). When God is left out of a life, that life has no balance staff to stabilize it; moreover, emptiness creates that vacuum which is indescribable and unexplainable. Augustine is often quoted for his classic expression: "Thou hast formed us for Thyself, and our hearts are restless till they find their rest in Thee."[1]

Yet individuals continue to pack material interests and activities into a crowded schedule;

some are seeking to escape that vacuum of God-loneliness. A movie actress, who possessed much of the fame and fortune afforded by that career, posed the following question as she was divorcing her husband: "Don't you think it is absurd to continue to exist without living?"

Brigitte Bardot was a French actress who was the sex symbol of the sixties and who made news with her three marriages and semipermanent boyfriends. At age thirty-eight she gave a newspaper the following evaluation: "I hate humanity. I am allergic to it. I see no one. I don't go out . . . I am disgusted with everything."[2]

Hobbs quoted Vanderbilt, the railroad king, as saying, "I have not had an hour's happiness in my life. I cannot eat or drink more than other men. I cannot wear more clothes. I require only one bed to sleep in. All the rest is the cause of perpetual trouble. My millions cause me ceaseless anxiety, day and night."[3]

Correspondingly, interesting and pathetic news circled around the richest man in the world, J. Paul Getty, who died in June, 1976, and who was considered by many of his friends as "the loneliest man in the world." A national magazine entitled its article about him: "The New Fears of J. Paul Getty."[4]

His seventy-four-room mansion at Sutton
Place, near London, included a thousand acres of
parkland, but it was patrolled by security men
and German shepherd dogs. Moreover, the win-
dows were barred with swordlike contraptions,
and the doors were kept locked. The interviewer's
account described his situation as follows:

> To the outsider, Getty seems imprisoned at
> Sutton Place. His fears—of flying, of being
> kidnapped, of spending money—keep him
> from traveling, from venturing out on the
> Surrey lanes around his home, from living
> even a gentle-paced jet-set life . . . .
> The richest man in the world is asked what
> single thing he would change if he had the
> power: "I'd change philosophy. People
> should be more content. The way to cure
> discontent is not necessarily to get more."[5]

Although Getty was married five times, the interviewer commented that "the sense of having
no one to fill his shoes is saddening Getty's old
age." "I built an empire," explained Getty, "but I
didn't build a family."[6]

The second factor in Cain's plight was his stub-
bornness in refusing to repent and to change
(Gen. 4:5). His omission of God from his life was

inward, probably not detectable to family observers if moral conduct was reputable. That inner set of mind began to harden. His angry disposition reflected itself in an outward display of sadness or sullenness. His attitude probably edged toward self-centered defensiveness. His reasoning could well have proceeded along these familiar lines: "I am satisfied with my offering; it's as good as anyone's. Nobody is going to force me to do anything. I'll do just as I please." Although God tried to reach him, Cain continued on the desperate course toward crookedness and ruin.

A third noticeable item describing the route to the wrecked life is recorded in Genesis 4:8. Outward expression of his inward rebellion led to murder. Cain, stubbornly determined not to change, decided to change others. He would remove the comparative element: Abel. Man's relationship to God is reflected by his relationship to his fellowman. The big self would chop down others in his attempt at self-esteem, satisfaction of security, and efforts of proving something to others.

So many people follow Cain's example of senseless viciousness. They seek to hurt or destroy others by means of criticism, gossip, or hateful activities. Life could be filled with delectable fruit, wholesome and nourishing, such as "... love, joy, peace, longsuffering, gentleness, goodness, faith, meekness [teachableness], temperance [self-control]" (Gal. 5:22-23). But some, like Cain, refuse to improve.

The progression in a sinful selection of life-style includes additional entanglement. While suffering the inward torrid torture of heated emotion, while displaying his depression by his countenance, and while being controlled by hatred that would produce murder, Cain engaged in cover-up efforts of lying (Gen. 4:9). Likewise, the history of sinfulness repeats itself even in our cultured civilization.

A fourth turn detected in the route to a ruined life is depicted in the threefold result which followed the rejection of divine compassion (Gen. 4:9-12). Fury, fright, and frustration filled the void of Cain's existence. Life had become warped, wrecked, and wretched. Its threads had been tangled and twisted. He lashed out in defensive accusations. The reader can soon discover reproduction of these qualities and actions in friends whom he loves.

Literally, Cain's declaration was "My punishment is greater than I can bear" (Gen. 4:13). The statement may be interpreted either of two ways.

He could have been complaining that divine punishment was too great to bear. Or, more probably, he was accusing God by stating that his sin was too great to be forgiven.[7] Several evidences concur to support the latter proposal. The Hebrew word *bear* (carry) is used frequently to denote forgiveness.[8] Again, God's efforts of rescue had revealed his interest in restoring Cain. But Cain's whole view had been that of resistance and denial of responsibility. His own interpretation of situations would have been warped like his mental health, attitude, and disposition. Moreover, guilt always seeks another to blame for failure.

Such lashing excuse-creation is normal for sinful humanity. People claim, "The Christian life is too hard to live. That's why I'm not a Christian." By accusing God of setting unreasonable requirements, individuals imply that they can be excused from guilt. Likewise, some complain, "Too many hypocrites are in the church. That prevents my accepting God's salvation." Whose fault is it? God's responsibility, perhaps, is to strike hypocrites dead. Or the church, perhaps the pastor, should protect the membership from falseness. The sinner's reasoning implies, at least, that someone other than he is to blame.

Another element of the proposed "threefold result" is Cain's unstable personality. His tortured, tangled, twisted life screamed in nervous insecurity (Gen. 4:14). Observe carefully the source of the charge about being driven out. Cain had already proved himself to be a liar, and God had not voiced any such penal conviction. The word translated "Nod" means "wandering."[9] It could depict his internal turmoil of aimless restlessness combined with his jittery traversing the countryside.

Twentieth-century citizens can easily identify with this aspect of Cain's predicament. Loud noise, loose living, constant conniving for activities, and tons of tranquilizing medications speak to the situation. As Cain charged Jehovah with responsibility, so people today shift it by saying: "It's just my weakness," or "I'm just made this way," or "God gave me these drives," or "Society warped me to be like I am." But the hurt remains. The condition worsens unless God is granted the privilege of restructuring and restoring the life.

The wretched result is disclosed further by the guilty conscience (Gen. 4:14c). Cain stated that everybody was against him, that everybody would torture him. To be pitied, indeed, is the poor, disturbed soul that must live with an aggravating, tantalizing, tormenting conscience. Its screams are deafening to the owner. Watkins wrote:

> The guilty conscience fears, when there's no fear,
> And thinks that every bush contains a bear.[10]

Shakespeare had Lady Macbeth to exclaim, "What, will these hands ne'er be clean? . . Here's the smell of the blood still. All the perfumes of Arabia will not sweeten this little hand. Oh, oh, oh!"[11]

Yet a fifth measurable mark in the route to a ruined life is indicated in Cain's determined departure from the presence of Jehovah (Gen. 4:16). Sad and pathetic to observe, it is, nevertheless, true that Cain refused to respond to Jehovah's pursuing love. His voluntary departure from the presence of Jehovah left him locked with his empty, vacuum self.

Still another factor, a sixth, remains an integral part of the ruined life: his sinful influence (Gen. 4:17-24). Too often interpreters have assumed the story closed with Cain's departure. Oh, that in this real life it could be true! The author first recounted how materially successful were Cain's descendants. Some were city builders (Gen. 4:17);[12] and some had flocks (Gen. 4:20), probably indicating wealth in both descriptions. Other favorable qualities included culture in music (Gen. 4:21) and skill in art or industry (Gen. 4:22).[13] Such an inheritance is commendable.

Values, however, are also transmitted in family relationships. Cain's emphasis on the material (without regard to Jehovah) was apparently contagious. Developments of sin weighed so heavily on the scales of character as to pronounce the descendants miserable failures in moral and spiritual character. Polygamy (Gen. 4:19), murder (Gen. 4:23), and haughtiness (Gen. 4:23) plagued their society. Oh, how tragic, but real—and so often repeated!

What does it take to build a worthwhile life? The following well-publicized, true experience suggests the need to include God and his character-building traits. In 1923, a very important meeting was held at the Edgewater Beach Hotel in Chicago. Among those present at this meeting were nine of the world's most successful financiers:

1. The president of the largest independent steel company

2. The president of the largest utility company
3. The president of the largest gas company
4. The greatest wheat speculator
5. The president of the New York Stock Exchange
6. A member of the Cabinet of the President of the United States
7. The greatest "Bear" in Wall Street business
8. The head of the world's greatest monopoly
9. The president of the Bank of International Settlements

Certainly, anyone would agree that the gathering included the world's most successful men. They had found the art of developing wealth and prestige. What did life, seen from the "end-zone," have for dividends to return them? Note the following history:

1. The president of the largest independent steel company, Charles Schwab, died bankrupt and lived on borrowed money for five years before his death.

2. The president of the largest utility company, Samuel Insull, died a fugitive from justice and penniless in a foreign land.

3. The president of the largest gas company, Howard Hopson, went insane.

4. The greatest wheat speculator, Arthur Cotton, died in a foreign land, insolvent.

5. The president of the New York Stock Exchange, Richard Whitney, was released from Sing Sing Prison.

6. The member of the President's Cabinet, Albert Fall, was pardoned from prison so that he could die at home.

7. The greatest "Bear" on Wall Street, Jesse Livermore, died a suicide.

8. The head of the world's greatest monopoly, Ivar Krueger, died a suicide.

9. The president of the Bank of International Settlements, Leon Fraser, died a suicide.

What waste in such wrecked, ruined lives when those men could have learned to live most successfully!

These insights from Cain's life help to explain the first question mentioned above: "What causes a person to do such things?" Now, let us seek evidence related to the second question: "Who did anything to prevent it?" God sought Cain step by step and offered his goodness at every turn.

The efforts of God to rescue Cain from the degrading direction toward a wasted and ruined life are enumerated in order to expose the persistent goodness of Jehovah for every person in the world. The first, basic divine contribution was that special, created element, "the image of God." Cain was granted that moral "God-shaped vacuum" as surely as was Abel. That natural desire for its Creator caused Cain to face his choices and respond to responsibilities. Eve apparently intended to indicate the spiritual nature of the child by two references.

First, it was seen in her choice of the word *ish* rather than *adam,* which refers to earthly, fleshly "man," or mankind generally. The matters of biological reproduction probably were understood by her during those months of gestation and the birth process. She undoubtedly knew that she and Adam produced the body; but she realized that there was more in that *ish* than "body-ness." Thus, in the second reference, she attributed Cain to "Jehovah." She surely used the expression "from Jehovah" or "with the help of Jehovah" to mean more than safety and assistance in the physical birth. Inasmuch as this is the first recorded use of the name "Jehovah" by a human being, she probably was defining the God whom she knew as the "Giver of Life." This would mean that he had given a distinctive quality different from *adam* (flesh). Therefore, the deduction can be stated that Cain possessed that "divine spark" (nature) that gave him moral and spiritual capacities equal to those of Abel. In this the goodness of God is evident.

The second exposure of divine love is the immediate attempt to reason and to elicit a favorable response from Cain (Gen. 4:6). Jehovah inquired into the cause of his dejection, not for information but for the purpose of leading him into personal examination of possible defects. Additionally, Jehovah stated the principle of divine righteousness (fairness) that if he would do right or make relationships right, he, too, would be accepted by God. Moreover, Jehovah continued efforts to achieve a rational evaluation by Cain in that Jehovah gave him information about the treacherous nature of sin. Jehovah depicted sin as an animal crouched at Cain's door, ready to devour. Such warning even magnifies the pursuing love of God. In addition, Jehovah attempted to stimulate the challenge to win by stating that Cain could rule over the sin. So many divine approaches in the early, more tender stage of the rebellious sinner declared the goodness of God to prevent the impending spiritual devastation.

Yet a third series of divine efforts of love are discovered after the murder of Abel. One approach that Jehovah tried was the emotional, family relationship. Note the repeated use of "brother" (Gen. 4:9-11). Jehovah must have known the value of keeping communication open, for he tried (by using questions) to get Cain to talk. Jehovah did not need to ask: "Where is Abel thy brother?" for information. But it could have opened the way for a normal confession (and the road to forgiveness). Likewise, the second question, "What have you done?" emphasized the seriousness of his situation so that Cain would repent.

Unable to register a favorable impression on Cain, Jehovah proceeded with a second, different approach after the murder incident. God revealed Cain's serious, cursed condition (Gen. 4:11-12). This divine diagnosis is interpreted here as a continuation of expressions of love in evangelism to cause this sinner to grasp his need for help from the source outside himself. Watts described it in these words: "The curse, it needs to be remembered, is a prophecy. It points here to the inevitable consequences of sin that must follow inasmuch as Cain refused to listen to God."[14] The diagnostic approach may be compared to other divine statements of warning for evangelistic purposes, such as the following: "The wages of sin is death" (Rom. 6:23), and "Cursed is every one that continueth not in all things which are written in the book of the law to do them" (Gal. 3:10).

Yet again in this series of appeals, Jehovah tried to touch a sensitive chord about a better life (Gen. 4:12). Comparison can be seen in John 10:10, also.

The tiring, tedious efforts of divine, persistent love made yet another spectacular provision of graciousness—the mark of prevention, security, and love (Gen. 4:15). The declaration of grace is introduced by a divine denial of Cain's wild, false charges of Genesis 4:13-14. The first words of God's answer may be translated "therefore" but, more probably "not so!" A difficulty in the Hebrew text involves two words which sound alike, but have a slight difference in spelling: *o* and *a*. Several manuscript evidences support the rendering "Not so," such as the Septuagint and the Vulgate. Plus, the context naturally leads to such a divine contradiction, and the interpretation is enhanced by the translation. Thus, even as Jehovah was forced to refute Cain's false accusations, he continued to express his love deliberately and explicitly. Hoping to convince Cain of that love, Jehovah declared a mark of protection prohibiting malicious torture by others against Cain.

The strain of spurned love, expressed by every possible means at every human experience-juncture, is sensed in the episode of this "route to a ruined life." One longs to witness the constructive reclamation in such a life as is graphically described by Myra Brooks Welch in the following poem:

THE TOUCH OF THE MASTER'S HAND

'Twas battered and scarred, and the auctioneer
Thought it scarcely worth his while
To waste much time on the old violin,
But held it up with a smile:
"What am I bidden, good folks," he cried,
"Who'll start the bidding for me?"
"A dollar, a dollar"; then, "Two!" "Only two?
Two dollars, and who'll make it three?
Three dollars, once; three dollars, twice;
Going for three—" But no,
From the room, far back, a gray-haired man
Came forward and picked up the bow;
Then, wiping the dust from the old violin,
And tightening the loose strings,
He played a melody pure and sweet
As a caroling angel sings.

The music ceased, and the auctioneer,
With a voice that was quiet and low,
Said: "What am I bid for the old violin?"
And he held it up with the bow.
"A thousand dollars, and who'll make it two?
Two thousand! And who'll make it three?
Three thousand, once, three thousand, twice,
And going, and gone," said he.

The people cheered, but some of them cried,
"We do not quite understand
What changed its worth." Swift came the reply:
"The touch of a master's hand."

And many a man with life out of tune,
And battered and scarred with sin,
Is auctioned cheap to the thoughtless crowd,
Much like the old violin.
A "mess of pottage," a glass of wine;
A game—and he travels on.
He is "going" once, and "going" twice,
He's "going" and almost "gone."
But the Master comes, and the foolish crowd
Never can quite understand
The worth of a soul and the change that's wrought
By the touch of the Master's hand.

MYRA BROOKS WELCH

7
Foundation of His Goodness: The Divine Names

Have you noticed the naturalness with which we change the use of names and titles of our God? An exciting adventure involves the discovery of meanings to be used discriminantly. How enriching is conscientious, understandable selection of descriptive terms for our Lord. Actually, our change of references to God in different situations or moods exhibits significance in each designation for deity. Psalm 18:1-2 dramatically reveals response to our spiritual needs by the numerous titles collected in one exclamation: "I will love thee, O Lord, my strength. The Lord is my rock, and my fortress, and my deliverer; my God, my strength, in whom I will trust; my buckler, and the horn of my salvation, and my high tower."

An observation of the way that we change references to God during prayer depicts the subconscious sense of our relationship with a distinctive aspect of his nature or character. Terms of salutation such as "Our gracious, heavenly Father" or "Holy Father" usually change to "Lord" or "Blessed God" in the progress of a prayer. References to "Father" seem to be expressed so naturally in private and sanctuary worship; whereas we naturally turn to terms like "Almighty God" relative to big projects, for example, when speaking of building programs or outdoor services in the context of creation's grandeur. Often we close with a different title: "In Jesus' name," "In our Redeemer's name," or "In the Savior's name."

One's devotional perspective is indicated by his use of terms: Supreme Being, Almighty, Lord, Master, Father, Jesus, Lord Jesus, Savior. Since each name or title for God has had tremendous impact upon the encouragement and influence of saints, we, too, can benefit devotionally by examining and enjoying their meanings.[1]

The use of a word for a name was considerably more significant to the ancients than to us. Biblical usage expresses character or history by a designation. Thus a change in character or history of a person (divine or human) would produce a change of name. Hence, certain revelation

from God or specific insight of man might call for
another name for God.[2]

Gustave F. Oehler focuses on this by the following explanation: "In short, God names Himself,
not according to what He is for Himself, but to
what He is for man; and therefore every self-
presentation of God in the world is expressed by a
corresponding name of God."[3] However, an all-
encompassing reference to the character of God is
also used in the word *Name*. See Psalm 8:1: "How
excellent is thy name in all the earth!"

Experiences in the life situation reveal qualities
of nature and character, both divine and human.
Thus a compilation of personality factors could
grant an evaluative examination relative to the
goodness of God. Some of these life-situation exhibits have occurred in association with various
names and titles for God. These can be highly instructive for our spiritual comprehension and
devotional enrichment.

This tremendous reservoir of spiritual resources is usually untapped because it is
unknown. Familiarity causes many devoted souls
to take for granted in actual use a variety of
names and titles. But few ever get the confidence
of inquiry: "What's in a name?"

The use of the very common word *name* in conjunction with a personal name, *Jehovah*, is exceedingly significant in Genesis 4:26 (ASV). For, the word *Jehovah* used alone began to be used in prayer. Furthermore, like a bright, illuminating star, careful observance of the exact Hebrew of Genesis 6:4 would aid in clarifying difficulties of interpretation relative to "giants," and alleged mythology. The "giants" were literally "men of *the* Name." Hence, the word *name* becomes a substitute for the personal name, "Jehovah."[4]

Early Christians conveyed the same kind of significance as their spiritual, Jewish ancestors in meaningful attachment to the personal name and titles of their God. This fact was so strong as to cause them at times merely to use the word *Name* with devotional flashback to their wonderful Lord (Acts 5:41; 3 John 7).

Because a name may describe qualities of a person, as sometimes does our nickname usage, "Tex," "Slim," "Red," Christians can eagerly stimulate devotional reflection. In this manner Matthew explained the purpose in the selection of the name "Jesus" because of its meaning: "for he shall save his people from their sins" (1:21). Names also generate an emotional response according to previous conditioning relative to them. When the name *Jesus* is singled out in reference to the one who is the *Savior* from man's great plight, spontaneous acclaim results. Examples are seen in popular gospel songs, such as the following:

Jesus is the sweetest name I know,
And He's just the same
As His lovely name,
And that's the reason why I love Him so;
For Jesus is the sweetest name I know.

LELA LONG

There is a name I love to hear,
I love to sing its worth;
It sounds like music in mine ear,
The sweetest name on earth.

FREDERICK WHITFIELD

Sweetest name on mortal tongue;
Sweetest carol ever sung,
Jesus, blessed Jesus.

WILLIAM HUNTER

The significance of a variety of names and titles for God is the truth of his self-disclosure with great meaning to those whom he encountered in different teaching circumstances. Emil Brunner wrote: "The communication of a name is the disclosure of one's self to the other, and thus the establishment—or at least the beginning—of a personal relation and communion."[5] The goodness of God is exhibited by continuing efforts to help mankind with such revelations of himself. As Oehler observed, "But this power of God within the world, and objective to man, is a name of God only in so far as it offers itself to be named by man and comes to him in the form of revelation, that is, in as far as man *can* know of it."[6] Oehler also noted a progressive accumulation that can prosper our understanding when he wrote: "In these stages the idea of God is so unfolded that the higher stages do not destroy the lower, but embrace them (1)."[7]

Devotional purposes are in evidence when spiritually-minded students perceive the relationships of names and titles to historical occurrences. Stone observed: "Now a name in the Old Testament was often an indication of a person's character or of some peculiar quality. But what one name could be adequate to God's

greatness?"[8] Correspondingly, rejoicing assurances spring from realization of his eagerness to
manifest the different aspects of his being and the
different relationships that he sustains to his
creatures. Summarizing these truths, Rees
stated:

> *The name* (shem) *of God* is the most com-
> prehensive and frequent expression in the OT
> for His self-manifestation, for His person as
> it may be known to men. . . . God is known by
> different names, as expressing various forms
> of His self-manifestation. . . . All God's
> names are, therefore, significant for the
> revelation of His being.[9]

8
Revealed by the Personal Name

Jehovah is the only personal name for the One True God in the Old Testament.[1] It occurs more than 6,700 times in the Old Testament.[2] This proper name is the one which so distinctly designates the One True God that the Jews could refer to him as the "Name" and be thoroughly understood.

Basic to his nature and to all the attendant attributes of his being is that this name was *personal*. "God," which translates "Elohim," is a title. A personal God can love, command, enter covenant relations, and so forth. Emphatic it is as Rees declared: "This is the personal proper name *par excellence* of Israel's God."[3] Contributing depth to our thrilling conviction, Knudson explained as follows:

> But the real significance of the name "Yahweh" does not lie in its meaning. It lies in the fact that it is a personal name. It distinguish-

es the God of Israel from all other dieties. He
is not one of a class but a distinct and separate
Being. He has an individuality, a definite character of his own. The very fact that he bore a
personal name emphasized this distinctness of
his personality.[4]

What more spiritual benefit can we derive from
understanding of the name, "Yahweh," in addition to his being a personal God and the tremendous devotional scope of that truth? When alert
for adopting insights of others' disclosure-
encounters, we can trace his enriching revelation.
These vital truths are entwined in the whole
knowledge of the true God revealed throughout
the Old Testament historical arena of experience-
disclosure, the person of Jesus, and our salvation
with attendant spiritual maturity.

Scholarly consensus recognizes that the name
is derived from the Hebrew verb root, "to be, to
live." But into that basic fact, much more content
is poured with each revelatory encounter.[5] Introductory to a chronological method of consideration for such explanation of "Jehovah," an
examination of Exodus 6:2-3 is appropriate.

The quotation from Jehovah is recorded: "And
God spoke unto Moses, and said unto him, I am
Jehovah: and I appeared unto Abraham, unto

Isaac, and unto Jacob, as God Almighty [El Shaddai]; but by my name Jehovah I was not known to them (Ex. 6:2-3, ASV).

Several significant factors attract our interest while interpreting Exodus 6:2-3. First, the word *know* is broad in scope. It is used regularly with a depth meaning of "experiential knowledge, real understanding, intimate knowledge," as in Hosea 4:1 referring to "knowledge of God." Also the verb is regularly used to express intimate relations, sexual intercourse, as in Genesis 4:1, 17. Correspondingly, the Greek word *ginosko* took such meaning, and it was used to declare that Joseph did not "know" Mary until the child was born. So, until Jehovah was able to make himself known in greater degree, that is, the great moral proclamation of Exodus 34:6-7, the earlier worshipers did not fully comprehend him by the name, Jehovah. Oehler explained the meaning of "Jehovah" in Exodus 6:3 by saying that it "*had not been yet understood* by the patriarchs, and that they had not the *full experience* of that which lies in the name (4)."[6]

Additional concerns indicate acquaintance and intelligent use of the name prior to the time of Moses. One is its use in the name of Moses' mother, Jochebed, meaning "Jehovah is glorious." Thus, it was cherished and used regularly. Yet another item concerns the context of the statement. With Moses' record in Egypt, plus the enormous task of being received genuinely by the Israelites, logic would rebel at the proposal of approaching them under a name quite unknown. A third insight is stated by Oehler in this way: "We have, *1st*, the occasional occurrence of the name Jehovah even in those parts of Genesis which belong to the Elohistic record, where the expedient of assuming an interpolation is altogether worthless."[7] Hence, the conclusion of pre-Mosaic origin and use of "Jehovah" is reasonable.[8]

What, then, did the special name mean to those who first explored its use? Eve is afforded the privilege of the first recorded expression of "Jehovah" (Gen. 4:1, ASV). The writer had reported activities of the God by "Jehovah Elohim," but he left it for Eve to use the personal name alone. She did so in relation to the birth of Cain. Reconstruct in imagination her intent, reflections, and expectations declared by the short, but profound statement: "I have gotten a man from Jehovah."

Avoid reading later knowledge of his meanness into his sweet babyhood. The first child ever to be born into the world brought a declaration about "Jehovah." She must have known of the mighty Creator God. She and the serpent both used the name "Elohim" to refer to him. She had experienced the bliss of beauty in the Garden with its divine-human communion. But, too, she had faced the judgment upon sin and the expulsion from the Garden. Her use of that special Hebrew word *ish,* meaning "person," translated "man," probably shows that she recognized a creative element in Cain, which only God can give.

She and Adam were responsible for the physical, *adam.* God had done more than aid her in gestation and delivery; he had provided the created, spiritual life of the baby. Her exclamation emphasized that the great Creator is immanent, interested in her concerns, and to be recognized as the "Giver of life" or "He who causes to be."[9]

The horror-filled experience of "going it alone" by human wisdom, strength, and decisions could well have brought Eve to realize the need for One who would be dependable and interested. "Jehovah" could well be defined from her statement as the supernatural Person on whom we rely for help. Apparently, she taught her two sons to worship him. Jehovah's persistent love, plus his righteousness, would be revealed in the episode to follow. More marvelous truths of "Jehovah" will unfold with other disclosure-encounters based upon this early foundation: One with us, dependably interested, able to provide!

There is intensified delight in this conviction concerning the personal aspect of Jehovah. This is enhanced by a logical, philosophical declaration by Emil Brunner:

> The God who is merely *thought* to be personal is not truly personal; the "Living God" who enters my sphere of thought and experience from beyond my thought, in the act of making Himself known to me, by Himself naming His Name—He alone is truly personal.[10]

> But the Name of God is only a "Proper Name" because it does not stand alongside of a general conception, of an appellation. The plural "gods" is an insult to God; it belongs to the Nature of God that there should be "none other beside Him." Therefore He cannot be known through general conceptions, but only through the naming of His own Name. The truly personal God is He who is not known through thought, but through the manifestation of His Name, the God of revelation.[11]

The expanding knowledge about the Person called "Jehovah" accumulates relative to sinful humanity exhibited by Cain in Genesis 4. "Jehovah" is the only name used throughout the delineation of God's efforts to reach that sinner. The love, already observed in "Jehovah," relentlessly pursued the rebel. Righteousness and love are equally demonstrated by "Jehovah" in regard to sin.[12] "Elohim" is not used in describing the events of Cain.

Jehovah was the name used for the God of worship (Gen. 4:26). To what degree Adam and Eve used it privately or taught it to their children in worship (offering, communion, and so forth), we cannot know. But, obviously, faith rather than doubt and surrender rather than disobedience were recognized as the primary, acceptable essential in "Jehovah" relationships.

Worship springs emphatically in the three experiences of life described in Genesis 4. First, the birth of a child turns attention toward "Jehovah," the Giver of life. In this experience man realizes his inadequacy. Second, the crushing efforts of sin, personally and socially, produce hungers for an adequate reliever (Gen. 4:13). Third, death creates a helpless sensation of human futility.

The naming of "Enosh" (Enoch) probably indicates the realization that physical death was to be a regular reality. Enosh more than likely means "weak or mortal one." Also, however, the fact that character qualities which are necessary for successful living exceed material and cultural achievements had been graphically demonstrated (Gen. 4:17-24).

To invoke the name Jehovah in worship was to see, in him to whom it was applied, both spiritual and moral sufficiency. And Eve used "Elohim" (Gen. 4:25) for the giver of Seth, identifying the one true Creator God with this "Jehovah" with whom they were accustomed to associate.

The selected list of descendants apparently indicates continued development in "Jehovah" worship as a primary objective for the writer of the book of Genesis, not merely a documenting of how things first began. That intriguing report of an ever-enlarging understanding of the marvelous qualities of "Jehovah" is a very profitable study.[13]

The personal name "Jehovah" was explained by God himself to represent the true God of moral essence in Exodus 34:6-7. This vital, remarkable quality distinguishes him from any god of the nations. Thus, the Hebrews could use the word

Name omitting even "Jehovah," and realize that
the reference was to this distinctive, unique deity.
Likewise, Christians enjoy employment of the expression "in the name of Jesus." Note the following evaluation of "Jehovah":

> *The most distinctive characteristic of Jeh,*
> which finally rendered Him and His religion ab-
> solutely unique, was the moral factor. In saying
> that Jeh was a moral God, it is meant that He
> acted by free choice, in conformity with ends
> which he set to Himself, and which He also im-
> posed upon His worshippers as their law of con-
> duct.[14]

9
Shown by the Unique Personal Presence

One of the foremost, enriching rewards awaits the Christian who will carefully engage in this particular study. Its exciting truths have scarcely been presented to the general Christian audience, although reliable scholars have reported them in specific contexts. Therefore, this collection of the data may provide both a devotional satisfaction and a spiritual hunger concerning this subject.

The special construction, "The Angel of Jehovah," designates a specific, divine person in Old Testament disclosure. Two interpretative factors have obscured this marvelous reality to the average Christian interpreter. One is the normal assumption that this One is identical with any angelic being who ministers the affairs of the sovereign God, that is to say, lack of observing the distinction. A second consideration, which naturally hinders the delightful discovery, is the "spiritualizing" of religious encounters in an effort not to be too literally physical or materialistic.

The conclusion of this investigation is stated at the outset to help the reader position his sights. "The Angel of Jehovah" is a peculiarly distinctive term for the same unique, divine person through the historical revelation of the Old Testament period. He is defined as being "Jehovah"; yet he is depicted as being separate from Jehovah. He performs what only God can do; yet he is visibly seen by people. When other designations are added to describe his activities, he is recognized as being the "Glory" (see Exodus; 1 Kings 8; Ezekiel), "the Holy One of Israel" (Isaiah), the Coming Ruler "whose goings forth" had already been observed in the past (Mic. 5:2). Have you ever noticed how the verse in Micah 5:2 is dissected, with the latter half being omitted in Christmas predictions? Thus, The angel of Jehovah is a manifestation of Jehovah on earth to the senses of people. When he was to be incarnated, he would be "Jesus."

In order to enjoy this realization, observe the reliable conclusion of the recognized, reputable scholars. A. H. Strong stated explicitly as follows:

(a) The angel of Jehovah identifies himself with Jehovah; (b) he is identified with Jehovah by others; (c) he accepts worship due only to God. Though the phrase "angel of Jehovah" is sometimes used in the later Scriptures to denote a merely human messenger or created angel, it seems in the Old Testament, with hardly more than a single exception, to designate the pre-incarnate Logos, whose manifestation in angelic or human form foreshadowed his final coming in the flesh.[1]

Accurate New Testament interpretation depends on notice of this reality. F. F. Bruce, commenting on Acts 7:29-34 (ASV) wrote:

The "angel" whom Moses saw (v. 30) was the special "angel of Jehovah" (Ex. 3:2)—*i.e.*, God Himself in His manifestation to men. In Ex. 3 the speaker is variously called "the angel of Jehovah" (v. 2), "God" (v. 4) and "Jehovah" (v. 7); so here the angel speaks with the voice of the Lord (v. 31), claims to be God (v. 32) and is called "the Lord" (v. 33).[2]

Furthermore, Bruce's explanation of Acts 7:37-41 includes the following insight: "The 'angel of the presence' of God (lit. the messenger of his face, Heb. *mal'akh panaw*) is the angel who makes

His presence real to men—in other words, the angel of Jehovah. . . .[3]

R. B. Rackham likewise based his understanding of Acts 7:53 upon this concept:

Thus (A) for JEHOVAH was substituted his Angel. This doctrine is indeed to be found in the OT itself. According to the OT, which S. Stephen quotes, it was *the angel of the Lord* which appeared to Moses in the bush. The angel of the Lord also appeared to Abraham, Hagar, and Jacob; and he was "the angel of the presence" who was with the Israelites in the wilderness. This angel speaks with *the voice of the Lord,* as God; and he is in fact, to use another name which had come into use, the Word of the Lord. . . . Stephen begins with *the God of glory.* The title is only found here: it is really *the God of the glory,* i.e. the Shekinah or "glory of the Lord"—the bright cloud of divine majesty which was as it were the pavilion of God himself. . . . It was then the very God who *appeared to Abraham.* How he appeared, S. Stephen does not say: but the word denotes a visible appearance. Probably he would have said in the person of his Angel."[4]

In similiar testimony, A. B. Davidson proposes

quite clearly the identification of "The Angel of
Jehovah" with "Jehovah" and that One as being
the Messiah who would come:

> This external manifestation of Himself is
> called the *Angel* of the Lord. . . . This Angel is
> not a created angel—He is Jehovah Himself in
> the form of manifestation. Hence He is identical
> with Jehovah, although also in a sense dif-
> ferent.[5]

It has not been uncommon to find in him a
manifestation of the Logos or Son of God, and
his appearance among men a pre-intimation of
the incarnation.[6] . . . Here regarding this Angel
two things are said: that Jehovah's name, *i.e.*
His revealed character, is in him; and that he is
Jehovah's face, *i.e.* the face of Jehovah may be
seen in him. They who look upon him look upon
Jehovah, and in him all that Jehovah is is present. . . . These passages indicate that in the
minds of those to whom this angel appeared, it
was an appearance of Jehovah in person.
Jehovah's face was seen. His name was revealed. The Angel of the Lord is Jehovah present in definite time and particular place. What
is emphatic is that Jehovah here if fully present.[7]

Exuberance abounds to the devoted Christian when the purposes and the consistency of our God through all the ages are found. Identifying this "angel of Jehovah" with Jesus, Davidson wrote extensively; a part of which is as follows:

> But one can readily perceive what Messianic elements lay in the idea of the Angel of the Lord,—who was at least a full manifestation of Jehovah in His redeeming power,—and how far the ancient Church was on right lines when it believed it could trace here the appearance of the Son of God .... further revelation has revealed that God manifested is God in the Son, and that it is not unnatural with the ancient Church to suppose that these preliminary theophanies of God in human form were manifestations of the Son, who at last was manifest in the flesh.[8]

Watts summarized the relationship of "Jehovah" and "The Angel of Jehovah" by saying: "They are identified in purpose, character, and work, but not in person."[9] Jesus declared: "He that hath seen me hath seen the Father" (John 14:9) and also: "I and my father are one" (John 10:30).

Interest can stimulate the observant student to

pursue the study within the Old Testament itself.
As one may carefully examine the record, he may
isolate the facts into three categories: (1) indica-
tions of identification of "Jehovah" and "The
Angel of Jehovah" as being one, (2) evidences of
their being separate persons, and (3) observations
of manifestation to the physical senses. The first
is discovered by the writer's using the names
"Jehovah" and "the angel of Jehovah" synony-
mously and interchangeably and by the Angel's
performing feats that only a divine person could
do, for example, give child, punish or forgive sin,
and perform miracles. The second category can be
noted when the Angel is reported as speaking to
Jehovah or as quoting Jehovah. The third is plain-
ly stated.

Selected Scriptures for such research are briefly
discussed to illustrate the proposed methods of
study. Note Genesis 16. "The Angel of Jehovah"
assumes the work of deity, and without doing so
as if quoting "Jehovah": (1) commanding Hagar
to return (v. 9), (2) promising to multiply descendants (v. 10), and (3) predicting Ishmael's future
(vv. 11-12). Yet, Hagar called the One talking to
her "Jehovah" (v. 13). Furthermore, she was convinced that she had *seen* God (v. 13).

Again, observe Genesis 18. "Jehovah" is

reported as being seen by Abraham throughout the chapter. Yet he proposed to exercise prerogatives of deity: to provide miraculously Sarah's child (vv. 9-15), to determine the destiny of Sodom and Gomorrah (vv. 17, 20, 32), and to claim to be "the Judge of all the earth" (v. 25, ASV). This One was a different person from "Jehovah" the sovereign ruler because Jehovah remained in his heaven, and because "no man has seen God at any time" (John 1:18, ASV), and because "God is a spirit" (John 4:24, ASV).

Similar studies can be made of Genesis 22, Genesis 32, Zechariah 1, Zechariah 3, and throughout the entire Old Testament. After these divine disclosures become understood, one can refer cautiously, avoiding reading into the passages, to the records of the relationship of "Jehovah" and his worshipers. For example, consider the Garden of Eden experience. Did Adam and Eve hear with their physical ears a sound of God walking? If their communion had always been in the spirit, would they think they could hide behind a material tree? Was this only anthropomorphic expression?

C. F. Keil wrote: "God conversed with the first man in a visible shape, as the Father and Instructor of His children . . . . This human mode of intercourse between man and God is not a mere figure of speech, but a reality.[10] Likewise, Leupold concluded:

> Besides, there is extreme likelihood that the Almighty assumed some form analogous to the human form which was made in His image. Nor is there anything farfetched about the further supposition that previously our first parents had freely met with and conversed with their heavenly Father.[11]

What purpose could be served for visible manifestations of God? Is not the spiritual communication as real as auxiliary evidences? Three possible explanations appear to be reasonable. First, God's intense interest in communication with mankind indicates his goodness by efforts. Keil concluded that the nature and limitations of humanity needed such manifestation.[12] Second, God's supreme revelation of himself by means of the incarnation of Jesus Christ suggests that temporary, visible appearances would be within his acceptable method of disclosure. Third, one might accept that God's normal procedure included being on earth, for the Holy Spirit (called Christ in you: Col. 1:27) is actively here in believers. This human living of the divine makes convincing evidence of understandable communication to the nonspiritually perceptive person. Thus, if one admits the "God with you" mode of revelation for the incarnation and the present Spirit operation, he can enjoy God's eagerness to reach mankind through theophanies of earlier history.

10
Disclosed by
Descriptive Titles

The significance of the terms *el* and *elohim* is in their usage as a title for "god." Both of them are used for the one true God and also for false gods. They are generally considered to be the oldest and most common designations for Deity. The etymology of each word is left in obscurity. The generally accepted root meaning of "El" is that of "strength, power."[1]

Scholars differ in conclusions relative to the relations of the two words. Rees apparently identified them, for he wrote: "One of the oldest and most widely distributed terms for Deity known to the human race is *'El*, with its derivations *'Elim*, *'Elōhim*, and *'Elōah*. Like *Theos*, *Deus*, and *God*, it is a generic term, including every member of the class deity."[2]

Some scholars believe that "Elohim" is an enlarged form, a plural of "El." Others consider

"El" to be an abbreviation of "Elohim." Some regard "Elohim" to come from a different root from "El" with a meaning of "fear, terror, One to be dreaded."[3] Andrew Jukes considered "Elohim" to be derived from a root meaning "to swear" and, consequently, described One who stood in covenant-relationship, ratified by an oath.[4]

The two terms seem to be used interchangeably, however.[5] Furthermore, they are used as a title, "God," not as a proper name, "Jehovah." Oehler wrote that Elohim "is not regarded in the Old Testament as properly a *name* of God."[6] Although Ringgren suggested that *'el* appears sometimes as a proper name,[7] he concluded that "'*Elohim* is above all an appellative."[8]

Moreover, in actual Old Testament usage, the reference to either seems to support an idea of "power." Ringgren concluded by stating, "At the same time, nothing in the linguistic use of these words opposes the assumption of an original meaning 'might, power.' "[9] Likewise, Watts wrote that Elohim "indicates the plenitude of power that inheres in the one God."[10] Elohim is used 2,570 times, describing "God," and "gods."[11]

Observation needs to be made that Elohim is a

plural form. Several explanations have been offered. Some authorities regard it as a relic of
polytheistic terminology. Others consider it to be
a clear indication of the Christian doctrine of the
Trinity. It probably refers primarily to the usual
Hebrew expression of fullness, plenitude, com-
pleteness by using plural words. To note its use
with singular verbs is quite interesting.

Girdlestone allowed some exceptions, but he
concluded that the combination predominately
referred to the true God when he wrote: "Although plural in form, the name is generally used
with a singular verb when it refers to the true
God."[12] Vos agreed, adding that when it was used
relative to pagan gods "it is always constructed
with a plural verb, whereas in a case of reference
to the true God it takes a singular verb."[13]
Likewise, Rees stated: "Its *form* is pl., but the
construction is uniformly sing., i.e., it governs a
sing. vb. or adj., unless used of heathen divinities
(Ps. 96:5; 97:7)."[14]

Thus, the delight for devotion results in that
the plural most probably describes the being of
magnitude, fulness, plenty of might, power, and
ability. Significance of this term is summarized
by Oehler as follows:

Elohim, as such, remains transcendent to the

world of phenomena; Jehovah, on the contrary, enters into the phenomena of space and time, in order to manifest Himself to mankind; a difference which appears at once in the relation of Gen. 1. 1 sqq. to 11. 4 sqq. This difference indeed, from the nature of the case, is not strictly kept up everywhere in the Old Testament in the use of the names of God. . . . But still it is shown . . . that the Old Testament writers had a very definite consciousness of the indicated difference.[15]

A scarcely noted fact relative to a discriminating use of "Elohim" is the definite article. Translations customarily omit it. The Hebrews apparently employed "Elohim" with or without the article to refer to their true God. Because they believed in only one real God, they could omit it. This is normally the case of Christians translating *ho theos* of the New Testament because they accept that he is the only one. There is, therefore, no need to require exactness of "The God."

When, however, an occasion for doubt might appear, they added that definite article to assure clarity of their conviction. During the wicked days after Cain's influence, the Hebrews employed the article to distinguish their God from the false deities which others had begun to worship. Thus Enoch walked with *The* God (Gen. 5:22, 24). The following list is provided for the student to pursue this relatively new discovery concerning use of divine names and titles.[16]

List of use of *The God* in Genesis

5:22, 24; 6:2, 4, 9, 11; 17:18; 20:6, 17; 22:1, 3; 22:9; 27:28; 31:11; 35:3, 7; 41:25, 28, 32; 42:18; 44:16; 45:8; 46:3; 48:15, 16.

II. COMBINATION WITH "ELOHIM"

Jehovah-Elohim

This compound name first appeared in Genesis 2:4. The author of the recorded events uses it. But it is not used by the early ancestors themselves. The term "Elohim" was used alone (and only it was used) in the primary creation account. The sovereignty and might of the Creator were qualities which needed to be emphasized. Yet when the author began to tell of Deity communing with Adam and Eve, he quite naturally turned to that personal name which indicated immanence, love, righteousness, faithfulness, and other such moral attributes. The author, living long after the first parents, would have possessed the accumulated treasure inherent in their understanding of the Name.

That one would relate the designation of the personal, immanent being with the Creator God of might and transcendence indicates deliberate skill for instructive purposes. He thus indicates that the Jehovah who communed and provided for earth's earliest inhabitants, and whom they worshiped, was the same person who with great power and intelligence created and developed the cosmic world. Their "Jehovah" was "God," the Supreme Deity of the whole universe. He was far more than a local, tribal god.

El Shaddai

This designation, "God Almighty," is used in that pivotal passage of Exodus 6:2-3. Consequently, students seek extremely rich possibilities in the title, but, nevertheless, must accept the reality of a confused diverseness of competent scholars concerning its origin and meaning. The term is used forty-eight times in the Old Testament of which thirty-one are in the book of Job.[17] It is rather remarkable that a general consensus obtains that it means "one who is able."

Three prominent derivations are usually advocated: the combination of two particles to mean "he who is sufficient," "breast," and "mountain." Girdlestone argued for the root meaning from a word meaning "breast" and signifying nourishment or bountifulness.[18] Stone followed Girdlestone's conclusion and illustrated the reasonableness of it by reference to idols of multiple breasts like Isis of Egypt and Diana of Ephesus. However, he also concluded that it meant that God had ability to provide sufficiently.[19]

Kelly accepted the view relating the origin to "mountain," but he also concluded that it meant a God capable to perform. He wrote: "It is thought by many that *Shaddai* means "mountain," thus *El Shaddai* would probably mean "Mountain One," or "God of the Mountain." It is a title describing him as the high God, one having power and majesty."[20]

An all-inclusive summary is presented in the following quotation:

Apparently, this rendering is based on an ancient rabbinic interpretation, *sha*, "who," and *dai*, "enough," i.e., "He who is self-sufficient" . . . . No fully satisfactory explanation of it has yet been accepted by all scholars. The term is usually explained as a cognate of the Akkadian word *Sadū*, "mountain," but not in the sense that *"El Shaddai"* would mean "God the Rock."

... Rather, "El Shaddai" would mean "'El-of-the-Mountain," i.e., of the cosmic mountain, the abode of *'El;* for the Patriarchs the term would mean "the God of Heaven."[21]

The same writer suggested that perhaps the history of the word included "breast," thus meaning "rounded" for the word came to be interpreted as "hills" or "mountains."[22]

The resultant force of "all-powerfulness" was indicated by the Septuagint (Greek translation) and by the Vulgate (Latin translation). Davidson reasoned that "the phrase *El Shaddai* may be simply an intensification of *El* itself"[23] Likewise, Watts, commenting on Genesis 17:1, concluded as follows:

> We may add that it is thus an intensification of Lord also, and emphasizes one side of the great combination Lord Yahweh. As such it fits, in a peculiar sense, the assurance of chapter 17 concerning the ability of Yahweh to give Abram a child in his old age.[24]

Devotionally stimulating is the contextual circumstances of the use of "El Shaddai" in Genesis. The first exposure appeared in that dramatic Genesis 17. Twenty-four years had elapsed since Jehovah first commissioned Abram and promised its fulfillment through his child. Attempt to relive his strain, struggle, and searching for evidences of its achievement. Two attempts to help God perform the task had failed: Eliezer (Gen. 15:2) and Ishmael (Gen. 16:2). Thirteen years had passed since the Ishmael proposal. What did Abram need to know as life continued to grow older with its ever reducing potential of reproduction? The God of power (El) would also be sufficient (Shaddai) to perfect his covenant. Thus, the distinctive description should energize steadfast faith.

Each divine-human encounter provides additional insights for the careful student. Therefore, the following titles are suggested for one's own research:

El Elyon = "God Most High," Genesis 14:22
El Ro'i = "God who sees," Genesis 16:13
El Olam = "God of ages," Genesis 21:33

III. COMBINATIONS WITH "JEHOVAH"

Adonai-Jehovah

Experience in the real world of accomplishments and conflicts provided the arena for discovering designations for God. Genesis 15 records another step in Abram's concept of Jehovah. The circumstantial background should be joined to events provoking a title for Jehovah from Abram, omitting the literary chapter division. Abram's courageous "commando" raid against five kings to rescue his nephew Lot did not settle the matters forever. They could very well strengthen their forces and retaliate. Could Abram survive?

Jehovah, ever alert to human quandary and question, assured Abram by saying, "I am your shield." Any future battles would not have to be fought in human resources only. In response, Abram joined the word (a title) "Lord, Master, Superior," to him whom he knew as his God, "Jehovah."

But Abram was concerned about a more significant factor of life than his survival. He was a man commissioned, entrusted with a worldwide responsibility of blessing through his seed (Gen. 12:1-3). But no heir was in prospect. And, with the real, definite possibility of annihilation by the revengeful kings, no child from him could be possible. Several years had passed since the divine promise of a child had been expressed. Yet the normal, natural processes of pregnancy had been inoperative. (Gen. 16:16 compared with 12:4 equals 11 years.)

Abram suggested a substitute within his relatives (Gen. 15:2-3) whom he could appoint to carry forth his mission. But Jehovah reassured Abram of personal fulfillment (Gen. 15:4-5). His response of surrender in faith evoked another utterance of "Lord, Master" with the precious, personal name, "Jehovah" (Gen. 15:8).

This title, similar to God, emphasizes sovereignty and corresponds to the New Testament use of *Kurios,* "Lord."[25] Watts described the meaningful use of this combination as follows:

"Lord," according to this context, describes the office or position of God: the transcendent, sovereign God who rules the universe and controls the events in the life of his people; in a word, the master of providence. The use of the two together reflects a conviction on Abram's part that the Lord's sovereign control of events in his life will be fulfilled according to the covenant promises of Yahweh. Together they give a surpassingly rich and practical view of God.[26]

The Hebrews continued to use this title. It is used 134 times alone, 315 times with "Jehovah" (only five times is the order reversed to read "Jehovah-adonai"), a total of 449 times.[27]

Jehovah-Jireh: "Jehovah will see and provide" (Gen. 22:14).

Recapture the struggle of faith which culminated in this experience-disclosure of God. That promised heir and the attendant prospect for accomplishment of that divine call had been realized after twenty-five years of waiting, longing, doubting, substituting, and trusting. Then—Abraham was called upon to present that child as a sacrifice. Could he possibly be understanding Jehovah's instructions correctly? How could he possibly ever have a replacement for Isaac? The account is emotionally dramatized with the expressions: "your son, your only son, whom you love," and "his son," and "my father."

Abraham, in surrendered confidence of trust, passed God's testing. And, Jehovah provided another sacrifice. Consequently, Abraham used another descriptive title for God: "Jehovah will provide."

Additional Titles

For one's further study in devotion, the following list of other such designations is provided:

Jehovah-Rophe = "Jehovah heals,"
                    Exodus 15:22-26
Jehovah-Nissi = "Jehovah, my banner,"
                    Exodus 17:15

Jehovah-M'kaddesh = "Jehovah who
                         sanctifies,"
                         Leviticus 20:8

Jehovah-Shalom = "Jehovah, source of peace,"
                         Judges 6:24

Jehovah-Tsidkenu = "Jehovah, our righteous-
                         ness," Jeremiah 23:5, 6

Jehovah-Rehi = "Jehovah, my shepherd,"
                         Psalm 23:1

Jehovah-Shammah = "Jehovah is there,"
                         Ezekiel 48:35

Notes

Chapter 1

1. Experience at Philippi, Acts 16.

2. Compare 2 Peter 3:18; 1 Peter 2:2; 1 Corinthians 2:1-3.

3. Note this differentiation translated in the King James Version, American Standard Version, *New American Standard Bible,* New Words Translations of the Holy Scripture, and J. Wash Watts, *A Distinctive Translation of Genesis* (Grand Rapids: Wm. B. Eerdmans Publishing Co., 1963), p. 20.

4. The Hebrew preposition, *Lamedh,* attached to an infinitive, customarily expresses purpose. Francis Brown, S. R. Driver, and Charles A. Briggs, *A Hebrew and English Lexicon of the Old Testament* (Oxford: The Clarendon Press, 1955), p. 517; E. Kautzch, ed., *Gesenius' Hebrew Grammar,* trans. A. E. Cowley (Oxford: The Clarendon Press, 1952), p. 348; and J. Wash Watts, *A Survey of Syntax in the Hebrew Old Testament* (Grand Rapids: Wm. B. Eerdmans Publishing Co., 1964), pp. 96-97. See also Genesis 2:15, "for the purpose of tilling it."

5. Observe that Adam's body was "formed" (existing dirt), Eve's body was "made" (literally, "build," existing rib), trees were "made" to grow out of the ground (2:9—existing potential), and cosmos "orderliness" was developed from matter "without form and empty"—1:1-2) by the Spirit of God's activity. See J. W. Lee, *Preaching from Genesis: The Perfecting of the Believer's Faith* (Grand Rapids: Baker Book House, 1975), pp. 12-13.

6. The technical, grammatical evidence for these keen distinctions is as follows. First, the term "create" is stated for bringing into existence a new item (matter; animal soul,

for example, "life principle"; and "image of God" in man). Second, after each statement of "creation" is a series of expressions, "let there be," which expresses the speaker's desire, but is not a command (not the Hebrew imperative form), and the desire so worded expects activity from forces other than the speaker, but cooperatively and supervised by God.

7. This conclusion is exhibited in the King James Version and the American Standard Version. And it is based on strong manuscript evidence adopted by scholars of the popular, critical Greek text, edited by Kurt Aland, *et. al., The Greek New Testament,* 2nd ed. (New York: American Bible Society, 1968), p. 551.

Since impersonal things cannot act to "work," God must in reality be the subject of the sentence. He works things for our good. Some ancient manuscripts so read and are followed by the Revised Standard Version, *New American Standard,* and Moffatt's translation.

8. The noun literally means "conspicuous," "in front of," or "opposite to." With the preposition it means "a help corresponding to him, that is, equal and adequate to himself" (Brown, Driver, and Briggs, *A Hebrew and English Lexicon of the Old Testament,* p. 617). See also J. Wash Watts, *A Distinctive Translation of the Old Testament,* pp. 21-33.

9. *The words ish* (man) and *isshah* (feminine) distinguish man as more than "earthly" as the *adam* is the Hebrew for "ground, earth, dirt." Male and female were both recognized with the very special term "create" in the spiritual capacity of "image of God" (Gen. 1:27). Eve used this new term *ish* to describe her first child; she considered him more than "flesh, earthly."

Chapter 2

1. Brown, Driver, Briggs, *A Hebrew and English Lexicon of the Old Testament,* p. 65.

2. Attention is directed to the dramatic style by different methods in the translations: a colon in the King James Version and American Standard Version, a dash in the Revised Standard Version, *Translation of Genesis,* a question mark in *The New English Bible,* an exclamation point in Moffatt's translation, and a series of dots in J. Wash Watts, *A Distinctive Translation of Genesis.*

This construction, *aposiopesis* (leaving a thought incomplete by a sudden break), is introduced with the particle *pen* which is used with a disapproving force in the conditional sentence.

Chapter 6

1. Williston Walker, *A History of the Christian Church* (New York: Charles Scribner's Sons, 1952), p. 179.

2. "Brigitte Bardot Says She's Bitter and Bored," *San Antonio* (Texas) *Express,* 19 February 1973, Sec. A, p. 15.

3. Herschel H. Hobbs, "Hands are for giving too," *The Beam,* October 1963, p. 41.

4. Joy Billington, "The New Fears of J. Paul Getty," *The Saturday Evening Post,* May/June 1976, p. 46.

5. Ibid., p. 47.

6. Ibid., p. 100.

7. For an excellent elaboration of evidence indicating this interpretation, see Watts, *A Distinctive Translation of Genesis,* note 6, p. 139.

8. Brown, Driver, and Briggs, *A Hebrew and English Lexicon of the Old Testament*, p. 671.

9. Ibid. p. 627.

10. W. Gurney Benham, *Poetical Quotations* (New York: Cassell and Company, Ltd., 1910), p. 40.

11. *Macbeth*, 5.1.4, 48-50.

12. "There were cities in this area at a very early date, and the remarkable statement of Genesis iv. 17 has been amply confirmed by the excavations," wrote Norman H. Snaith, *The Distinctive Ideas of the Old Testament*, p. 28.

13. John R. Sampey, *The Heart of the Old Testament* (Nashville: Sunday School Board of the Southern Baptist Convention, 2nd ed., 1922), p. 23.

14. J. Wash Watts, *Old Testament Teaching* (Nashville: Broadman Press, 1967), p. 23.

Chapter 7

1. Interest in this subject was first stimulated by studies of the Old Testament with Watts, *Old Testament Teaching*, "Critical Problems Number IV: Variation of Divine Names" p. 25. "Is there any spiritual lesson in the variation of divine names in Genesis 1:1 to 4:26?"

2. Geerhardus Vos, *Biblical Theology: Old and New Testaments* (Grand Rapids: Wm. B. Eerdmans Publishing Co., 1954), p. 76. Also G. H. Parke-Taylor, *Yahweh: the Divine Name in the Bible* (Waterloo, Ontario: Wilfrid Laurier University Press, 1970), pp. 1-4.

3. Gustave Friedrich Oehler, *Theology of the Old Testament*, trans. and ed. George E. Day (Grand Rapids: Zondervan Publishing House, reprint ed., n.d.), p. 124.

4. Because the serious student might want to study

passages in which translations do not observe these distinctive appellations, he could locate specific identification in biblical references by using a concordance that transliterates the Hebrew. *Analytical Concordance to the Bible* by Robert Young is one such resource. Many translations use the term "Lord" for several of these designations.

Also, Parke-Taylor devotes an entire chapter to the use of "The Tetragrammaton Within Christianity" in his book, *Yahweh: The Divine Name in the Bible*, pp. 97-109.

5. Emil Brunner, *The Christian Doctrine of God: Dogmatics*, trans. Olive Wyon (Philadelphia: The Westminster Press, 1950), p. 123.

6. Oehler, *Theology of the Old Testament*, p. 124.

7. Ibid., p. 87.

8. Nathan J. Stone, *The Names of God in the Old Testament* (Chicago: Moody Press, 1944), p. 7.

9. *International Standard Bible Encyclopedia*, which see, "God," by T. Rees.

Chapter 8

1. The hybrid term "Jehovah" is used in this material because it has become generally naturalized by extensive usage as referring to a distinctive Being. Readers would acknowledge that it is a combination of consonants of one Hebrew word and vowels of yet a different. An excellent enlarged explanation can be found in J. Wash Watts, *A Distinctive Translation of Genesis*, pp. 136-38. Similar accounting was made by Albert C. Knudson, *The Religious Teaching of the Old Testament* (New York: Abingdon Press, 1918), pp. 54-55.

The basic four consonants, YHWH, are called

"Tetragrammaton," Greek word for "four letters." The following summary is recorded in *Encyclopedia Judaica*, which see, "God, names of."

At least until the destruction of the First Temple in 586 B.C.E. (Before Common Era) this name was regularly pronounced with its proper vowels, as is clear from the *Lachish Letters, written shortly before that date. But at least by the third century B.C.E. the pronunciation of the name YHWH was avoided, and Adonai, "the Lord," was substituted for it, as evidenced by the use of the Greek word *Kyrios,* "Lord," for YHWH in the Septuagint, the translation of the Hebrew Scriptures that was begun by Greek-speaking Jews in that century. Where the combined form 'Adonai YHWH occurs in the Bible, this was read as 'Adonai 'Elohim, "Lord God." In the early Middle Ages, when the consonantal text of the Bible was supplied with vowel points to facilitate its correct traditional reading, the vowel points for 'Adonai with one variation—*a sheva* with first *yod* of YHWH instead of the *hataf-patah* under the *aleph* of 'Adonai— were used for YHWH, thus producing the form YeHoWaH. When Christian scholars of Europe first began to study Hebrew, they did not understand what this really meant, and they introduced the hybrid name "Jehovah."

2. G. Johannes Botterweck and Helmer Ringgren, ed., *Theological Dictionary of the Old Testament,* trans. John T. Willis (Grand Rapids: Wm. B. Eerdman's Publishing Co., 1974), p. 64. Others stated the number specifically to be 6,823 in Stone, *The Names of God in the Old Testament,* p. 18, and Parke-Taylor, *Yahweh: The Divine Name in the Bible,* p. 4.

3. *International Standard Bible Encyclopedia*, which see, "God," by T. Rees. Supporting the statement are Botterweck and Ringgren, ed., *Theological Dictionary of the Old Testament*, 1:64; Knudson, *The Religious Teaching of the Old Testament*, p. 54; and Parke-Taylor, *Yahweh: The Divine in the Bible*, p. 4.

4. Knudson, *The Religious Teaching of the Old Testament*, p. 57.

5. Scholars often propagate investigation of the usage of names to determine the source (documents or oral tradition) of these materials. Some conclude that no distinctive, devotional differences were intended nor are now available. Other equally competent scholars proceed with research evidence to believe that the basic names were known and used interchangeably with purpose. Excellent research is available in introductory studies of the Old Testament, encyclopedia articles, and other sources. Compare R. K. Harrison, *Introduction to the Old Testament* (Grand Rapids: Wm. B. Eerdmans Publishing Co., 4th printing, 1974), pp. 3-82, and *Theological Dictionary of the Old Testament* by Botterweck and Ringgren (vol. 1).

6. Oehler, *Theology of the Old Testament*, p. 97. See also Norman H. Snaith, *The Distinctive Ideas of the Old Testament* (New York: Schocken Books, 1964), p. 135, which records, "This word *know* means more than awareness, for the root *y-o-'* (know) in Hebrew has a personal as well as an intellectual meaning."

7. Ibid.

8. Vos, *Biblical Theology*, p. 130: "The statement need mean nothing more than that the patriarchs did not as yet possess the practical knowledge and experience of that side of the divine character which finds expression in the name.

'To know' in the Hebrew conception and the same word in our every day parlance are two quite different things. The context of Ex. 6:3 even renders probably that a practical, experiential knowledge is referred to."

9. See Watts, *Old Testament Teaching,* p. 24 and Oehler, *Theology of the Old Testament,* pp. 95-96.

10. Brunner, *The Christian Doctrine of God,* p. 122.

11. Ibid., p. 123.

12. A fuller treatment displaying the goodness of God in persistent love is presented later in these materials. But these moral factors are mentioned here because of their inherent nature with the name "Jehovah."

13. This initial study of the name "Jehovah" in early Genesis was given to depict his natural goodness. Additional, explicit evidence of that name can be enjoyed by personal research in the following suggested references. The call of Moses indicates the "Jehovah" of faithful dependability (as true to the past patriarchs, so he would continue to be to Moses and Israel), holiness (ground with his presence), love (deliverance in response to knowing their suffering), and personal involvement all synchronized quite genuinely. Moreover, "Jehovah"—the God of Covenant—maintains similar relationships to us (Abraham, Genesis 12:1-3; Israel, Exodus 19:5-6; and believers, Exodus 34).

14. *International Standard Bible Encyclopedia,* which see, "God," by T. Rees.

Chapter 9

1. Augustus Hopkins Strong, *Systematic Theology,* reprint edition (Philadelphia: The Judson Press, 1943), p. 1166. See also, J. Hardee Kennedy, *The Commission of*

Moses and the Christian Calling (Grand Rapids: Wm. B. Eerdmans Publishing Co., 1964), p. 20.

2. F. F. Bruce, *Commentary on the Book of Acts,* (Grand Rapids: Wm. B. Eerdmans Publishing Co., 1955), p. 151, footnote 49.

3. Ibid., p. 152, footnote 54. Compare also Exodus 19:8-20; 33:11; and 34:5.

4. Richard Belward Rackham, *The Acts of the Apostles* (Grand Rapids: Baker Book House, 1964), pp. 101-102.

5. A. B. Davidson, *The Theology of the Old Testament* (New York: Charles Scribner's Sons, 1922), p. 116.

6. Ibid., p. 296.

7. Ibid., pp. 297-98.

8. Ibid., pp. 298-99.

9. Watts, *Old Testament Teaching,* p. 81.

10. C. F. Keil and F. Delitzsch, *The Pentateuch* in *Biblical Commentary on the Old Testament,* trans. James Martin, 3 vols., reprint ed. (Grand Rapids: Wm. B. Eerdmans Publishing Co., 1949), 1:97.

11. H. C. Leupold, *Exposition of Genesis,* 2 vols. (Grand Rapids: Baker Book House, 1953), 1:155.

12. Keil and Delitzsch, *The Pentateuch,* 1:97.

Chapter 10

1. Note Brown, Driver, and Briggs, *A Hebrew and English Lexicon of the Old Testament,* pp. 41-42; Oehler, *Theology of the Old Testament,* p. 87; and Vos, *Biblical Theology,* p. 77.

2. *International Standard Bible Encyclopedia,* which see, "God."

3. Oehler, *Theology of the Old Testament,* p. 87; and Vos, *Biblical Theology,* p. 77.

4. Andrew Jukes, *The Names of God in Holy Scripture* (Grand Rapids: Kregal Publications, published 1888, reprint ed. 1967), p. 18.

5. Botterweck and Ringgren, ed. *Theological Dictionary of the Old Testament,* 1:272; and *Encyclopedia Judaica,* which see, "God, names of."

6. Oehler, *Theology of the Old Testament,* p. 126, footnote 2.

7. Botterweck and Ringgren, ed., *Theological Dictionary of the Old Testament,* 1:273.

8. Ibid., p. 276. Also, Davidson, *Theology of the Old Testament,* p. 38.

9. Botterweck and Ringgren, ed., *Theological Dictionary of the Old Testament,* p. 273.

10. Watts, *Old Testament Teaching,* p. 4.

11. Botterweck and Ringgren, ed., *Theological Dictionary of the Old Testament,* 1:272; Stone, *Names of God in the Old Testament,* p. 7; and Parke-Taylor, *Yahweh: The Divine Name in the Bible,* p. 4. Robert B. Girdlestone, *Synonyms of the Old Testament* (Grand Rapids: Wm. B. Eerdmans Publishing Co., reprint ed., 1970 of the second ed. 1897), p. 19, reports its occurrence as 2,555 times.

12. Girdlestone, *Synonyms of the Old Testament,* p. 19.

13. Vos, *Biblical Theology,* p. 78.

14. *International Standard Bible Encyclopedia,* which see, "God."

15. Oehler, *Theology of the Old Testament,* pp. 98-99.

16. Acknowledgment is given to J. Wash Watts, *Glimpses of God in the Yahweh God of Genesis* 1-11 (Nashville:

Seminary Extension Department, Southern Baptist Convention, 1957), pp. 94-95.

17. Jukes, *The Names of God in Holy Scripture*, p. 66; and Stone, *The Names of God in the Old Testament*, p. 34.

18. Girdlestone, *Synonyms of the Old Testament*, pp. 32-33.

19. Stone, *The Names of God in the Old Testament*, pp. 34-36.

20. Page H. Kelly, "The Old Testament Concept of Covenant," *Outreach* 6 (July 1976), 28.

21. *Encyclopedia Judaica*, which see "God, names of."

22. Ibid.

23. Davidson, *Theology of the Old Testament*, p. 40.

24. Watts, *Old Testament Teaching*, p. 42.

25. *International Standard Bible Encyclopedia*, which see, "God."

26. Watts, *Old Testament Teaching*, p. 41.

27. Botterweck and Ringgren, ed., *Dictionary of the Old Testament*, 1:62.